Morgan Hill Country School
Spring 2000
Scholastic Book Fair

This book donated to

The Library

by

Book Fair

ATHLETES

THE PERFORMERS

Kyle Carter

The Rourke Press, Inc.
Vero Beach, Florida 32964

Edited by Sandra A. Robinson

PHOTO CREDITS
© Kyle Carter: cover, title page, pages 8, 10, 17, 21;
© Frank Balthis: pages 4, 7, 12, 13, 15, 18

ACKNOWLEDGMENTS
The author thanks the Minnesota Twins Major League Baseball Club
and the Chicago White Sox Major League Baseball Club for their
cooperation in the preparation of this book

Library of Congress Cataloging-in-Publication Data

Carter, Kyle, 1949-
    Athletes / Kyle Carter.
    p. cm. — (The Performers discovery library)
    Includes index.
    ISBN 1-57103-061-1
    1. Sports—Juvenile literature. 2. Athletes—Juvenile literature.
[1. Athletes. 2. Vocational guidance. 3. Occupations.] I. Title.
II. Series.
GV707.C355   1994
796—dc20   94-12386
                                                        CIP
Printed in the USA   AC

TABLE OF CONTENTS

ATHLETES

An athlete is a person who is trained and skilled in sports. A skilled athlete has strength and **stamina,** and can move quickly and easily.

People do not usually grow up to be full-time athletes. Most people leave the long hours of practice behind after high school or college.

A very few, very talented people, however, continue to be athletes as adults. They are the **professional** athletes, people who are paid to play.

Professional athletes are highly skilled

KINDS OF ATHLETES

Almost all professional — pro — athletes are talented in more than one sport. However, they usually choose to play the sport they do best.

Pro athletes in America play football, baseball, basketball, soccer, golf, hockey or tennis. Professional athletes also box, run, skate and take part in several other sports.

A few athletes, such as Gene Conley, Bo Jackson, Danny Ainge and Deion Sanders, have played two different professional sports.

Professional athletes are often talented in several different sports

LEARNING TO BE AN ATHLETE

People usually discover their athletic talent at an early age. Adults help them develop with coaching and encouragement.

Youngsters often play several sports. As children grow older, they spend more time on the sports they do or like the best.

High school and college athletes often play no more than two or three sports at the **varsity** level. The best athletes at large universities usually play just one sport.

On-the-field coaching helps young
athletes learn soccer and other sports

COACHING

Coaches are the adults who teach young athletes the skills to play a sport. Coaches also **motivate,** or encourage, athletes to work and play harder. A coach wants each player to reach his or her **potential** — to be as good as he or she can be.

Athletes are coached at each step of their athletic journey. Even professional athletes learn from coaches.

A Major League baseball coach trains infielders and outfielders

Women compete in professional sports such as golf

Distance runners have to be in excellent condition

PRACTICE MAKES PERFECT

Practice is part of every athlete's training program. Coaches plan practices to help athletes improve their skills and stay "sharp." They use practice times to help athletes prepare for their next competition, or game.

Many athletes also practice on their own, without being asked or told to. Athletes know that keeping good practice habits will help them keep their skills sharp.

Practice prepares bicyclists for cross-country competition

CONDITIONING

Conditioning is how athletes "tune" their bodies. Conditioning is training that includes physical workouts, or exercises, and eating the right foods. Workouts build athletes' stamina and make them stronger. Workouts also help an athlete's body become more flexible.

Professional athletes condition themselves by lifting weights, running and stretching. Each sport has a different conditioning program.

Stretching helps condition athletes, like these Major League baseball players

THE ATHLETE'S WORKPLACE

Imagine being in a huge **stadium** surrounded by over 50,000 spectators, or viewers. A stadium is an athletic field surrounded by high walls, with row after row of seats for spectators. For many professional and college athletes, a stadium is their workplace.

Athletes have other workplaces, too. Athletes change clothes in a locker room. They leave the locker room to practice or play in a gym or on a playing field.

An athlete's workplace may be a huge stadium, like the Rose Bowl in Pasadena, California

IN THE BIGS

Almost everyone who participates in sports would like to be a pro. Becoming a pro is a very exciting goal, but one that is tough to reach.

Think about the 28 teams in Major League baseball. On Opening Day each April, just 700 men have a job playing on those big league teams.

Careers may not last long for the talented athletes who make "the bigs" — the big leagues. Injuries end many careers. Advancing age takes most other athletes out of professional sports before they are 40.

Playing in the major leagues of a sport is the dream of many young athletes

CAREERS IN ATHLETICS

A person can make a career of athletics without being a professional athlete. You might want to coach. You could also work in sports as a trainer, or doctor. Other careers in sports are sports writing and broadcasting on radio and television.

The chances of being a pro athlete are tiny. There are many more athletes than there are pro careers. However, everyone can enjoy sports for fun, competition and exercise.

Glossary

conditioning (kun DISH en ing) — the process of staying ready to compete through exercise and careful eating habits

motivate (MO tih vate) — to excite, encourage and inspire someone to work or play hard

potential (po TEN shul) — the best that a person can possibly be or do

professional (pro FESH un ul) — referring to a person who is trained and paid for doing a job

stadium (STAY dee um) — a field for sports surrounded by walls and rows of seats

stamina (STA min uh) — endurance; the ability to keep working or playing for a long time

trainer (TRAY ner) — in sports, someone who takes care of the minor injuries and athletes' conditioning

varsity (VAR sit ee) — the best team that a school or college enters in athletic competition with another school or college